SYMBOLISMS

T. CARL WHITMER

BOSTON
RICHARD G. BADGER
THE GORHAM PRESS
1909

Copyright 1909 by T. Carl Whitmer

All Rights Reserved

THE GORHAM PRESS, BOSTON, U. S. A.

In the interest of creating a more extensive selection of rare historical book reprints, we have chosen to reproduce this title even though it may possibly have occasional imperfections such as missing and blurred pages, missing text, poor pictures, markings, dark backgrounds and other reproduction issues beyond our control. Because this work is culturally important, we have made it available as a part of our commitment to protecting, preserving and promoting the world's literature. Thank you for your understanding.

CONTENTS

The Grinding	7
The Earthen	11
Interlude: The Cycle	16
The Mother	18
World Rest	20
The Darkening	22

SYMBOLISMS

THE GRINDING

"TWO WOMEN SHALL BE GRINDING AT THE MILL; THE ONE SHALL BE TAKEN AND THE OTHER LEFT".

Two women—middle aged—in Eastern costume. Both are grinding at mills. They speak:

ONE.
    I love.
THE OTHER.
    I hate.
ONE.
    We grind
        And grind
THE OTHER.
    Early and late.
ONE.
    I love; you hate.
THE OTHER.
    Yet we grind
        And grind
            Both alike.
                And
                      Both wait.

ONE.
>	Yet we grind
>>	And grind
>>>	Although I love.
>	I love;
>>	You hate.

>	I see now in the clouds (*pointing*)
>>	A little spot.

THE OTHER.
>	(*Looks below toward the sea.*)

ONE.
>	(*Eagerly*)
>	There is a greater spot in the clouds;
>>	It is as a mighty hand!

THE OTHER.
>	(*Calmly*)
>>	I look to the sea.

>	Nothing is there but
>>>	A foam!

ONE.
>	I see God!

THE OTHER.
>	I see nothing;
>>	But I hear the wind.

ONE.
>   (*affrighted*)
>> I see God in the cloud!
>>> I see—Him!!

(*listening*) I hear Him now! (*eagerly*)
THE OTHER.
>   I hear the wind
>> And the foam dash
>>> And the waves.

>>> And now the bird-scream!

ONE.
>   (*quietly*)
>> O sweet God!
>>> (*She disappears*)

THE OTHER.
>   I hear the wind
>> And the foam-dash
>>> And the waves.

>   You (*pointing above*) loved.
>   I hate.
>   I—am alone.
>   I—wait!

>   I hear the wind
>> And the Waves.

(grinding)
    But I must grind
        And grind
            Early and late.

I grind
    And grind.

Grind,
    Grind
        And
            Wait!!

II
THE EARTHEN

"Then shall two be in the field; the one shall be taken and the other left."

THE YOUNGER.
    (*to himself*)
        I love.
THE OLDER.
    (*to himself*)
        I hate.
THE YOUNGER.
    (*to* THE OLDER)
        We work
        And work.
THE OLDER.
    (*bitterly*)
        And wait
        And—wait.

THE YOUNGER.
    Why do you work?
THE OLDER.
    To keep three lives in
              Hate!

>And you?

THE YOUNGER.
>The day comes sooner.

THE OLDER.
>But night is softer;
>Night is sweeter.

THE YOUNGER.
>I long for the day.

THE OLDER.
>(*starting his plough*)
>>I hate the light!

THE YOUNGER.
>(*eagerly*)
>>An Angel
>>>Is in my furrow.

THE OLDER.
>(*with a curse*)
>>Rocks and earth—only!

THE YOUNGER.
>The Angel beckons.
>>(*spurring on his oxen*)
>>>Yes, I come.

THE OLDER.
>(*He tries to hurry his oxen. Then finding they will move no faster, he says:*)
>They cannot move faster.
>>(*stopping them*)

                    There!
            What do you see?
(*Running towards* THE YOUNGER)
                            Tell me,
            What do you see?
THE YOUNGER.
      (*looking upwards*)
            I come!

      Ah! I knew Thy arms
            Were gentle.
(*He disappears. His oxen stand by the furrow.*)
THE OLDER.
      (*looking towards the sky*)
            Nothing but a
                  White Cloud!

(*He goes to the oxen of* THE YOUNGER)
            Your oxen have seen the Angel.
                  I will look into their eyes;
                        And I, too,
                              I shall see!

      And I will yoke
            Thine to mine
                  And they shall draw together.
                        Early and late

     Will I work;
   And—O God—
     Wait!

(*He leads the oxen to his own. They plough.*)
  Perhaps I shall see what
      He saw.
   There! (*His own oxen stumble.*)
 No, it is a rock.

    (*They stumble again.*)
  They draw not well.
   (*He lashes them and gives an oath.*)
(*mutters*)
   Rocks! Rocks!
     (*He lashes them again and mut-
      ters his curses.*)
   You loved;
     I *hate*.
   I work
     And work
       And—
 I hate the light.
   I hate the—
     (*curses*)

   To keep three lives
 In—hate!
 I work

    Early and late.
Work
    Work
        And
            Wait!!

III

INTERLUDE: THE CYCLE

A night;
    Stars and the moon;
        A wind;
            A sheet of light;
          A dawn;
              A Day.

When the golden haze is last upon the autumn leaf;
When the birds upon the boughs, wrapped within that burning color, cease their songs;
When the grinding of labor is done;
When the horses of the ploughmen see God;
When the world revolving in inconceivable space disintegrates and becomes new Force;
When mortality is robed in the spaceless, uncrushable immortality;
When bodies change into pulses;
Then again come

A night;
    Some stars;
        A moon;
            Leaf odor;
Gentle winds;
    Grayness;
        Dawn;
            Color;
                A flash;
                    Day;
                        The Eternity!—

IV

THE MOTHER

"The children are come to the birth; and there is not strength to bring forth."

(A woman lies in a bed. Her husband is in the shadow of a distant corner.)
WOMAN speaks:
    Come to my side, Dear,
        And wait; not from yonder.

Come (*gasps*)—to—my—side.

  Look! (*gasps again*)
     Can—you—(*pointing upwards*)

  (*Her head falls back.*)

    (*reviving*)
         I see the child—that I—

      I see it———with God!

And now,
    God reaches out His arms for me.

So you beckoned me
    When you loved me to be near——
                      And I came.

Shall I not go to———Him?

   I am going away
         Slowly———
              Slowly———

O God, may he not come?
            Call,
                Call him!

WORLD REST

"The strong men shall bow themselves."

Two men at the edge of a wood
  THE ONE talks:
    Yonder, Majji, is the sun;
    But it shall not last.
    And the grass on the side of the hill:
      See! It is growing brown even now.

    The sun shall be no more;
    The moon and stars are near their end;
    The world is going to its rest.

    The faint light you see
    Is the sun's last effort.

    I hear another song, Majji!
    It is the voice of a woman.
    I thought we had heard
            The last voice.
    The world is near its end.
         Soon—
                (Majji is taken)

  Majji!
    Where have you gone?
    Where the sun's light is?
    Where the stars are?

I am ready, too;
    I am ready.

 (*eagerly*) Majji!

VI

THE DARKENING

"AND THOSE THAT LOOK OUT OF THE WINDOWS BE DARKENED."

Near a wood. A man and a woman stand within a latticed window. The sun is obscured by a light mist which gradually becomes thicker and thicker, first brown and then a reddish black.

THE WOMAN:
    (*Sings in a low voice. Then a silence. She turns to the man and says:*)
    The sun is almost gone.
    No light upon your face, Dear.
    Ah! one ray is left.

    Put your arms about me;
    Draw my head to your breast;
    We can love but a moment.
(*They stand in silence*)

I see a Hand
    In the darkness of the cloud.
        It is an Angel's.

I Hear a Voice!

VOICE:
    I am Gabriel that
      Stand in the
          Presence of GOD!)

It calls you, now, Sari.
(Sari disappears)
I see the Hand again
In the blackness of the cloud.
It is beckoning for me.

I am ready.

Come,
    Come and take me
        To my Beloved.

Yours arms are gentle.

    Gentler,
      Softer,
        Sweeter than
            I knew.

    GOD!

Printed by Libri Plureos GmbH in Hamburg, Germany